WITHDRAWN

Ace
Your Creative Writing Project

by Dana Meachen Rau

Enslow Elementary

an imprint of

Enslow Publishers, Inc.

40 Industrial Road
Box 398
Berkeley Heights, NJ 07922
USA

http://www.enslow.com

The author would like to thank Kelly Sanders, Literacy Specialist, West District School, Farmington, Connecticut, and Christie Wall, Third-Grade Teacher, Lake Garda School, Burlington, Connecticut, for the helpful conversations during the writing of this book.

Enslow Elementary, an imprint of Enslow Publishers, Inc.

Enslow Elementary® is a registered trademark of Enslow Publishers, Inc.

Library of Congress Cataloging-in-Publication Data
Rau, Dana Meachen, 1971–
    Ace your creative writing project / Dana Meachen Rau.
        p. cm. — (Ace it! Information literacy series)
    Includes bibliographical references and index.
    Summary: "Find out where writers get their ideas, your story's characters and
setting, writing, revising, and presenting your writing"—Provided by publisher.
    ISBN-13: 978-0-7660-3395-5
    ISBN-10: 0-7660-3395-3
    1. Creative writing (Elementary education)—Juvenile literature. I. Title.
LB1576.R37 2009
372.62'3—dc22
                                        2008024888

Printed in the United States of America

10 9 8 7 6 5 4 3 2 1

To Our Readers:
We have done our best to make sure all Internet Addresses in this book were active and appropriate when we went to press. However, the author and the publisher have no control over and assume no liability for the material available on those Internet sites or on other Web sites they may link to. Any comments or suggestions can be sent by e-mail to comments@enslow.com or to the address on the back cover.

❣ Enslow Publishers, Inc., is committed to printing our books on recycled paper. The paper in every book contains 10% to 30% post-consumer waste (PCW). The cover board on the outside of each book contains 100% PCW. Our goal is to do our part to help young people and the environment too!

Cover photo: Associated Press/Image Source
Interior photos: Alamy/Image Source Pink, p. 9; Alamy/Design Pics, Inc., p. 24; Corbis/Peter Mountain/Warner Bros/Bureau L.A. Collection, p. 16; Corbis/JLP/Jose L. Pelaez, p. 22; Corbis/Tim Shaffer/Reuters, p. 27; Corbis/Ron Chapple Stock, p. 42; Getty Images/Josef Fankhauser/The Image Bank, p. 7; Getty Images/AsiaPix, p. 32; iStockphoto.com/Andres Peiro, pp. 3, 5, 11, 17, 25, 33, 41; iStockphoto.com/lillis photography, p. 34; iStockphoto.com/morganl, p. 37; iStockphoto.com/Bonnie Jacobs, p. 41; Jupiter Images/Thinkstock Images, p. 4; Photo Edit/Mary Kate Denny, p. 8; Photo Edit/Michael Newman, p. 10; Photo Edit/David Young-Wolff, p. 30; Photolibrary.com, p. 14; SuperStock/Brad Walker, p. 21.

Contents

Are you ready to do some creative writing? Put on your backpack and start collecting ideas!

1

Collecting Ideas in Your Backpack

Imagine that you are wearing a backpack as you walk through the woods. You're on the lookout for fun items to collect. Maybe you find a bumpy brown pinecone. Over there you spot a star-shaped leaf. Under a log is a glittery rock that looks like a jewel.

Collecting writing ideas is just like collecting items in a backpack. As a writer, you are always wearing an invisible backpack. Every experience you have, every person you meet, and every place you go can be an idea for creative writing. You can store these ideas in your backpack. Then they are handy when you need them.

Creative writing is any writing that is meant to entertain readers. There are three main types of creative writing:

1. A personal narrative tells about an experience in your own life.
2. A fiction story is a story you make up.
3. A poem has many forms. Poets try to use words in a creative way to communicate a feeling or idea. They might tell a story or describe an object in simple words. Some poems have rhythm and rhyme, like a song.

Authors choose the best type of creative writing to share their ideas. For example, imagine that you want to write about a garden. In a personal narrative, one sentence might go like this:

The yellow sunflowers grew taller than me!

This sentence could be part of a fiction story:

The fairy queen's throne was on top of the tallest sunflower in the yard.

And these could be lines from a poem:

Tall flower
Round and yellow
Like a bright shining sun

Are you ready to get started? Collect everyday experiences in your backpack. Don't worry if you've never met the president or won an Olympic medal. Small experiences make good ideas, too. You can write about walking your dog across a field. You can tell a funny story about a disastrous attempt to do laundry.

Look for some new experiences. If someone asks you to go rock climbing, give it a try. You might love it! Your first climb could make a great story. Even if you hate it, that would be a great story, too! Every experience you collect could be used for a personal narrative.

Also be sure to fill your backpack with something that every writer carries— imagination. You could turn your real experiences into fictional ones. Maybe instead of walking a dog, you're taking your pet dragon for a walk!

Every new experience gives you writing ideas. How about rock climbing?

Let's say you want to write a poem. Reach into your backpack and find one item or moment. A worn baseball glove or a beautiful day at the beach can give you lots of details to describe.

The Scary Blank Page

You wouldn't think an innocent piece of blank paper could be scary. But it can be terrifying for a writer without any ideas! Here are some ways to get your creativity flowing.

Make a List

One word can lead to an idea. Write down ten words that pop into your head. Then go back and circle the one that is most interesting to you. Maybe you wrote down *pretzel* because you're hungry. Why not write about the biggest pretzel in the world?

Apples and Oranges

Two words can also lead to an idea. Compare and contrast two different things. How is your grandfather like a marshmallow? Maybe he's soft and sweet. That might make a funny poem.

What Are They Thinking?

A picture can lead to an idea, too. Flip through magazines with pictures of people. Think of them as characters. Ask yourself questions about what they might be saying. What do you think their lives are like?

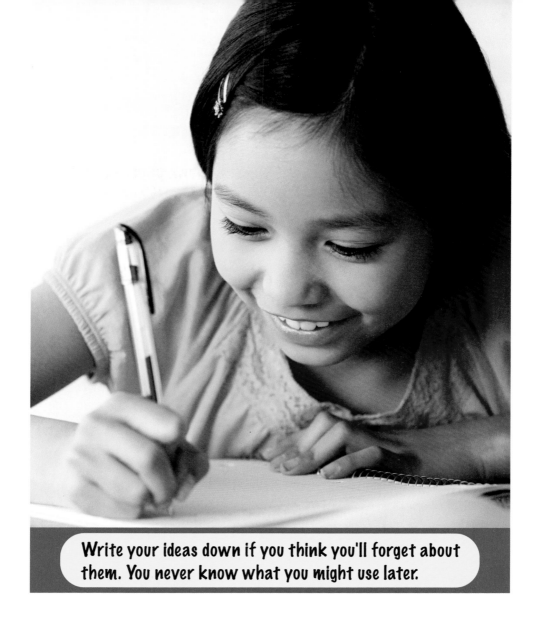

Write your ideas down if you think you'll forget about them. You never know what you might use later.

Not every writer meets the same people, goes to the same places, or does the same activities. Every writer works a little differently. As you keep reading this book, though, you'll see that all writers follow a similar process from idea to finished piece.

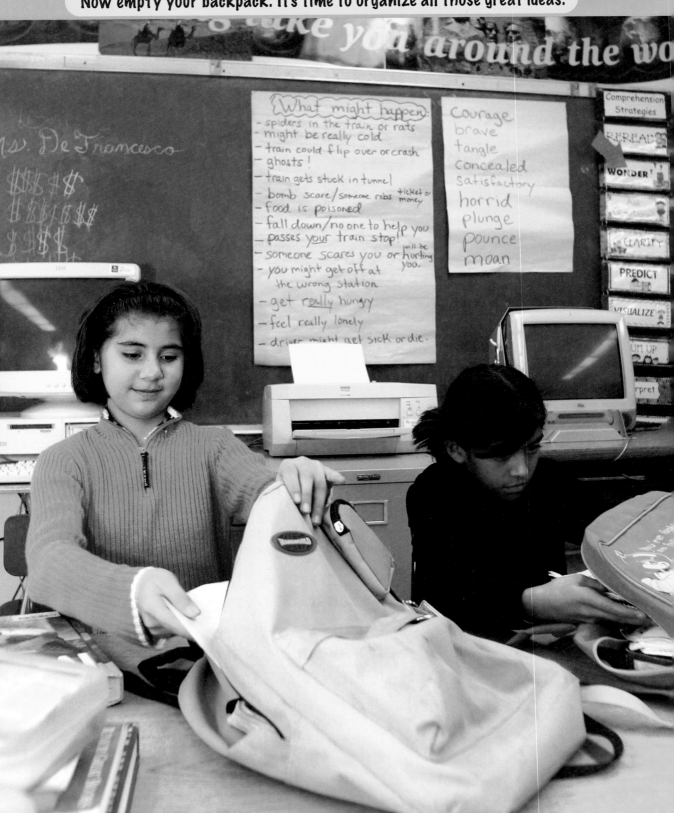

Unpacking Your Ideas

It's time to dump out your backpack. You have a pile of great ideas to share. Now you need to put them together for your reader.

Many writers start this process by asking themselves a question. They ask, "What's the best way to share my idea?" Do you want to describe a rainbow you saw yesterday? A poem might be the best form of creative writing to use. Use personal narrative to tell about the time you lost your kite in the park. An idea about a squirrel who wants to play baseball might work best as a fiction story.

Narratives, stories, and some poems need characters, a setting, and a plot. Characters are *who* is in the story. The setting is *where* the story takes place. The plot is *what* happens in the story. Your piece also needs a beginning, a

11

middle, and an end. All types of creative writing must include details.

You can start your piece by prewriting. Prewriting is making a writing plan. (The prefix *pre-* means "before," so *prewriting* means "before writing.") A great way to begin is to use graphic organizers. A graphic organizer is like a picture. It helps you organize your thoughts.

Let's say you want to write a personal narrative about getting ready for a party. A problem and solution chart could help you make your writing plan.

Problem and Solution Chart

Problem	Solutions	Result
My guests were arriving for a party in an hour, and nothing was ready!	—wrapped towels on my feet to wash floor while I decorated —gave baby brother streamers to unroll —had older brother blow up balloons —frosted cake with one hand, set table with other hand	The doorbell rang, and I finished just in time!

For a fiction story, you can use a 5W chart to plan your characters, setting, and plot. Don't worry about writing complete sentences. Just write a few words that will help you remember your ideas later.

5W Chart

Who? (characters)	an alien boy and his dog
Where? (setting)	in outer space
When? (setting)	in the morning
What? (plot)	can't get home in time for school
Why? (detail)	their spaceship is broken

As you prewrite, it is important to think about the theme of your piece. Your theme is your main message. What do you want readers to learn from your story or poem? For example, what would be the theme of a personal narrative about your first day at a new school? It could be "bravery," or maybe even "fear." Let's say you're

A Venus flytrap catches its lunch. You could write a scary poem about a moment like this!

planning a poem about a Venus flytrap eating an insect. This poem might have the theme "Be careful!"

Not all writers make a prewriting plan. Some just start drafting. Jane Yolen, a famous children's author, says, "I generally do not think out plots or characters ahead of time. I let things roll along. . . . I want my own writing to surprise me."[1] Remember, though—Jane Yolen is a professional author. She has been writing for a long time. For beginning writers, prewriting is really useful. It can help you check that your story has all the important parts, or that your poem says everything you want it to say.

As you write down your ideas, your plan will take shape. It's okay if your first draft is messy. At this point, don't even worry about perfect spelling. After you have a draft, you'll go on to revising. Revising is when you add words, take words away, and change details to make your piece better. One draft is never enough, even for famous authors. Award-winning author Gail Carson Levine believes that "the best way to write better is to write more."[2]

The Writer's Process

Writers often follow these steps:

1. Prewriting: **organizing your thoughts and making a writing plan**

2. Drafting: **creating the first version of your story, narrative, or poem**

3. Revising: **making your piece better**

4. Peer review: **getting feedback from other writers**

5. Publishing: **sharing your work with readers**

Roald Dahl created memorable, wacky characters in his book *Charlie and the Chocolate Factory*. This picture is from a movie version of the book.

Who and Where: Characters and Setting

Characters can be people, like Charlie Bucket in *Charlie and the Chocolate Factory* by Roald Dahl. They can also be animals, like Stumpy the Squirrel in Cynthia Rylant's *Gooseberry Park*. Characters can even be objects, such as Frosty the Snowman, or something in nature, such as the clouds in Eric Carle's book *Little Cloud*.

The narrator of a story is the person telling the story. The narrator may be a character in the story—but not always. In a personal narrative, *you* will probably be both the main character and the narrator. For a fiction story, you make up your own narrator and characters. You get to choose names for them. You also decide how they look, act, and feel. Poems may have characters, too. Shel Silverstein, the poet who wrote *Where the Sidewalk Ends,* often writes poems with characters.

If you need character ideas, check your backpack. Characters can be based on people you know. They can be based on strangers, too. Author Kate DiCamillo says, "Writing is seeing. It is paying attention."[3] Why not sit on a park bench and watch families go by? Ask yourself questions as you watch. Why is that boy in such a hurry? What made that girl laugh so hard? Then you can make up stories to answer your questions.

Open your backpack again. Look through your ideas and experiences to find details about your characters. Some writers "interview" their characters. They create a character sketch. A character sketch helps you get to know who you are writing about.

In your creative writing, try not to just *tell* readers what a character is like. It is boring just to tell your reader, "Henry was a smart boy." It is better to *show* your characters' personalities. Write about what a character actually says and does. For example, dialogue can show your reader what your characters are like. If your character says, "Out of my way!" you are showing that he is gruff and bossy. But if your character says, "Excuse me, please. Do you mind moving aside? I need to get by," he is polite and respectful.

Also show your characters' behavior—what they *do*. "Veronica was hungry" might be true. But instead, try

Character Sketch

Use these questions to write details about your characters. Copy the questions onto a separate piece of paper and add your answers.

- Name and age of my character:
- What does my character look like?
- What does he or she like to do? What does he or she *not* like to do?
- What is my character's favorite color, book, food, song . . . ?
- Who are my character's friends?
- What do other people think of my character?
- What does my character keep in his or her desk at school?

"Veronica shoved the cookie into her mouth in one bite. Then she took a gulp of milk before she even finished chewing." In the second example, you are *showing* your reader that Veronica is hungry. You never even have to use the word *hungry*.

Here's an example from a personal narrative. It only *tells* the reader how the narrator feels:

Even though I am growing up, I still care about the stuffed bear I slept with when I was a baby.

19

Your writing will be much better if you show the feeling through words and actions. Here is a revised example:

I was cleaning my room when I spotted my stuffed bear on the floor. I picked up Scoobers and straightened his blue bow. "You poor thing!" I said. "I'll find a better spot for you!" I cleared a place next to my science books and sat Scoobers on the shelf near my bed.

This example *shows* instead of *tells* readers that the narrator cares about his bear.

Setting is where and when your narrative, story, or poem happens. Look in your backpack. Take out your collection of all the places you've been. Maybe you spent a vacation on a ranch or went camping in the woods. Other settings could be school, your bedroom, and even the inside of a car. You can also wonder about places you've never seen but want to visit—like Egypt, or the Moon. Try to imagine a place long ago in history—like a Spanish castle or a steam train headed west.

As you plan your setting, think about the mood you want to create. The mood is the feeling that your reader gets from your writing. If your setting is a spooky cave, use words that make it sound spooky. Don't describe how the walls are brown or rough. Instead, talk about the silent shadows and the dark corners.

Your setting can be as far away as Egypt—or as nearby as your living room.

As you add details, don't just think about how the setting looks. What about your other senses? Use a graphic organizer to brainstorm for setting details.

Also ask yourself *when* your piece takes place. Are you writing about what happened to you last summer? Then your setting is in the past. The present means the story is happening right now. Are you writing about what life will be like in a hundred years? Do your characters wear hover sneakers and use robots to do their homework? Then your setting is the future!

Setting Brainstorm

Setting: _My sleeping bag_

I see _the blue plaid pattern_.

I hear _the swishy sound it makes when I move_.

It smells _musty like my basement where we store it_.

I taste _the s'mores I ate before bed_.

I feel _the silky fabric on the outside and the soft flannel inside_.

Ask an adult to help you with Internet research.

Research: Filling Up Your Backpack

The setting of your writing might be sometime in history. Or you might want to write about something scientific. This means you'll have to do some research. Head to the library. Take out books about your topic. You can also do research on the Internet. When you use new information, you have to be careful to write it in your own words. Plagiarism is taking someone else's words or ideas and calling them your own. Plagiarism is against the law.

When you do research online, you have to be careful. A teacher or other adult can help you decide what sites are safe for you to visit. If a Web site asks you to enter any personal information—such as your name, age, address, or photograph—go to another site.

Get Tense!

It is important to think about the tense of your verbs. The time of your story—the past, present, or future— will help you figure out what tense to use.

Past tense:

Charlie <u>ate</u> hot dogs for dinner last night.

Present tense:

Charlie <u>eats</u> hot dogs for lunch.

Future tense:

Charlie <u>will eat</u> hot dogs for dinner—if there are any left!

Exciting events keep us interested in a story. The events of a story are called the plot.

Chapter

4

What's the Story?

Your characters and setting may be thrilling, but you need a good plot, too. Your reader will lose interest if nothing really happens! A story's plot has a beginning, a buildup, a climax, and an ending. Most stories have a central problem that the main character tries to solve.

Beginning

A good story starts with a bold beginning. First, you need to make your readers want to read more. Then you have to provide some background. In the beginning, you will introduce your characters and the setting. You should also introduce the story's main problem.

Here is an example of a story's beginning. It tells us what the story will be about, but it doesn't make you want to keep reading:

One day I got a new bike.

25

You can spice up a beginning by using dialogue. For example, show your character's feelings right away:

"That's the one!" I shouted, as I ran up to the blue ten-speed bike.

"Hmmm," Dad said. He looked at the price tag. "Two hundred dollars, Karina."

I hung my head. No one could afford that!

In this beginning, we meet the characters—an excited girl and her not-so-excited dad. We see the setting—a bike shop. We also know the problem—Dad is sure to say no to Karina. This beginning leaves the reader with more questions. What will Dad say? Will Karina get the bike? If so, how will they get the money? Readers will want to find out the answers.

Starting in the middle of the plot can also be a good way to pull readers right into the scene:

Tyler raced as fast as he could toward home base. The coach waved him in, but the other player was rushing closer with the ball, ready to tag him.

Look at how much we learn in just two sentences. Already we know the main character (Tyler), the setting (a baseball game), and the problem (getting home in time).

A baseball game can turn into a fantastic story. Just think of all the events in one game!

Buildup

In the buildup of your story, your character tries to solve the problem. You can do this by building suspense. Suspense is when you can't wait to find out what happens. For example, let's say your main character is worried that his friend will never call. That's his problem.

The phone rings, but it's his grandmother. It rings again, and it's his cousin. It rings again, but it's his dad. Readers will be in suspense as they wait for the call along with the character.

Climax

The climax is the most important or exciting moment of the story. At the climax, the reader finds out how the problem gets solved. For example, a climax could be when a rescue crew arrives to save a group of lost hikers. Or the main character finally scores a goal to win the soccer tournament in overtime. Take time to describe this moment. Help your readers picture the action as it happens.

Perhaps a character named Riley has been trying to think of ways to cheer up her sick brother Sam. She's tried everything—chicken soup, a stuffed animal, and a homemade card. The following example is the climax of this story. But it is not very exciting.

Sam just wanted Riley to keep him company.

Take some time to make the moment more exciting. Have Riley sit down on Sam's bed. Describe the quilt. Then describe how Riley feels and what she says to Sam. Describe Sam's expression and what he says to Riley. Show how much they care about each other by the way they act.

Ending

A story might not be over after the problem is solved. In the ending, we learn what happens after the climax. Don't end the story too quickly. The events of the story have probably changed your main character. Tell your readers how your character feels, or what your character will do with the lesson she has learned.

The following ending doesn't show what your character experienced in the story:

I put on my pajamas and went to bed.

This ending shows the reader that the character has definitely changed:

As I went to bed, I thought, "I will never try to dress up my dog in doll clothes again!"

Poetry doesn't always have a plot. Some poems just describe something, such as a character, setting, object, or moment. Like personal narratives and fiction stories, poems also have themes and moods. But poems often use fewer words than other types of writing. With just a few words, poets create a picture in a reader's mind. Some poems may only be two lines long. Others may have two hundred lines! Personal narratives and fiction stories use paragraphs to break up the story. Many poems use groups of lines called stanzas.

A young poet makes a collection of her work.

Rhyme, rhythm, and repetition can really spice up a poem. Rhyme is the use of the same sound in more than one word, such as *bake* and *cake*. Rhythm is when lines have a particular beat, like music. Repetition means using the same words over and over.

Open the box.
I can't wait!
Open the box.

This is gonna be great!

Open the box.
What's in there?
Open the box.

It's full of air!

> There is repetition of the phrase "Open the box!"

> The words *wait* and *great* rhyme.

> If you read the poem aloud, you can feel the beat. This is the poem's rhythm.

30

Haiku for You!

Haiku is a type of poetry that has a few rules. The whole poem can only have seventeen syllables—five in the first line, seven in the second line, and five in the third line. A syllable is how many sound parts a word has. For example, *cat* has one syllable. *President* (pres-i-dent) has three syllables. A haiku often describes nature. But this short poem can describe anything, even a mug of hot chocolate.

1	2	3 4	5		5
White marshmallows float					
1 2 3	4	5 6	7		7
On a thick brown cocoa pond					
1	2	3 4	5		+ 5
Warm and sweet to drink					
					17

Don't be afraid to make big changes to your writing. This is what revision is all about.

Making It Better: Revision

Revision is the most fun part of creative writing. It is like playing with modeling clay. Everything you need is there—the characters, setting, and story. But it is just a blob. With revision you can make it into something readers can understand.

One way to revise is to add details. This is called expanding your writing. You also revise by taking out words. This is called tightening. Finally, you can replace some words with better ones. Revising means making your piece the best it can be.

First, look for places to expand with details. Teacher and writer Barry Lane says that detail "is the best tool any writer has to bring writing into focus and find deeper meaning."[4] You might have a picture in your head as you write. Did you give enough detail for your reader to see the same picture?

Maybe you wrote a personal narrative about your trip to the candy store. You included this sentence:

I saw lots of candy.

This is a good place to add more details to describe the candy you saw. Ask yourself questions. What types of candy did you see? What did the candy look like? How did you feel about the candy? This expanded description is better:

The store was filled with hundreds of kinds of candy. Some lollipops were bigger than my head. I saw gummy bears, gummy worms, and gummy sharks. They had the sour balls that fizz when you suck on them—the ones my brother likes. They even had some rocks made of chocolate!

Details can also tell you more about a character. Don't just

Your words can make readers feel like they can smell, taste, and touch something . . . like candy in a store.

add any details, though. You always have to think about the mood and theme of your piece of writing.

This sentence doesn't tell us much about the character or what he is going to say:

The principal stood in front of the room. He had something to tell the children.

Details can tell us more about the principal. Here is an example with more details:

The principal wore a red tie and blue pants. He had a silver watch and wore glasses. He stood in front of the room. He had something to tell the children.

The details above don't tell us about the principal's personality or his news for the children. If you add the right details, readers learn a lot more:

The principal stood in front of the room with his arms folded at his chest. He glared at the children.

With just a couple new details, we have a scary principal with bad news to share. Other details create the opposite picture:

The principal rushed in and waved to the children. He had a huge smile on his face as he stood in front of the room.

Now we've created a friendly principal with good news to share!

As you revise, you decide the best way to tell your story. Are you only using characters' thoughts to tell the story? Or will the characters speak to each other in dialogue? Many good stories have a mixture of both. Let's say your story includes this sentence:

Gabby forgot to put the lid on the blender before mixing up some grape juice.

Revise this section by using dialogue instead.

"Could you hand me the grape juice?" Gabby asked.

Max gave her the jug. "What do you need it for?"

"I want to put it in the blender," she said.

"Do you think that's a good idea?" Max asked.

"We won't know until we try!" Gabby pressed the button.

"You forgot to put the top on!" Max exclaimed.

"Could you hand me a towel?" Gabby asked.

This dialogue tells us what Gabby is doing and what Max thinks about it. The writer doesn't say Gabby makes a mess. But we know she does because she asks for a towel.

You can use special writing techniques to make your writing more colorful. Comparing two unlike things is one way. Venn diagrams can help you make comparisons. Perhaps you wrote a story about how crazy your classmates are. When you revise, think about what you could compare them to. Maybe a bunch of monkeys?

Venn Diagram
Monkeys Compared to the Kids in My Class

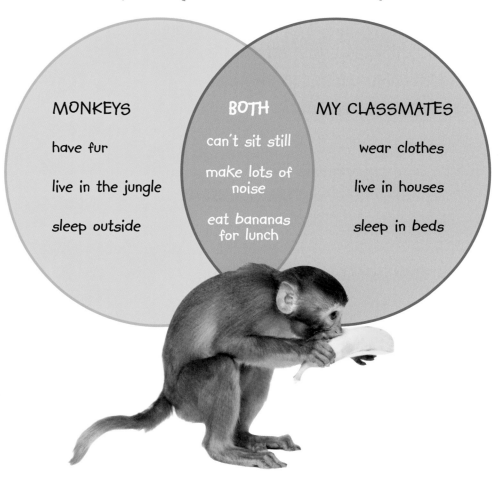

MONKEYS

have fur

live in the jungle

sleep outside

BOTH

can't sit still

make lots of noise

eat bananas for lunch

MY CLASSMATES

wear clothes

live in houses

sleep in beds

Similes are comparisons using the word *like* or *as*. For example, "My noisy classmates chattered like a bunch of monkeys" is a simile. A metaphor compares two objects without using *like* or *as*. "Joe is a monkey on the playground" is a metaphor.

Helpful Writing Techniques

Alliteration: repeating the first sound in a word
Snakes slither silently.

Personification: talking about an object as if it is a person
The leaf danced in the wind. (The leaf is dancing like a person. Leaves don't really dance.)

Hyperbole: exaggerating the truth
This line must be 60 miles long!

Poets often use similes and metaphors:

Spaghetti's swirly
curly
twirly
like a bowl of ········· (**simile**)
wiggly worms.

Warily
I wind my fork
In the bowl of worms ········· (**metaphor**)
Wiggling in spaghetti sauce.

Adding words can help make your writing more fun. But tightening is important, too. Take out unnecessary words, sentences, or images. If they are not important, they are probably in the way. As a writer, you always make choices. Decide on the main idea of each scene. Then decide if all the details in that scene relate to your idea. For example, this writer wanted the action to be fast. She needed to keep up the pace. You can see where she deleted some words.

The ~~large wooden~~ ship rushed toward the shore ~~of the island~~. ~~The island had palm trees, green grass, and black rocks~~. The captain had to steer clear of the rocks, or the ship would crash. ~~He ran around the deck and shouted out orders~~. He grabbed the wheel and pulled hard ~~to make the ship turn in the other direction~~. The rocks rushed closer ~~as wind blew on the sails and sent the boat toward the rocks~~. The crew scurried on deck and pulled down the sails. With one last yank, the captain turned the boat ~~away from the shore~~. A rock scraped the ship, but it ~~only left a long line along the side and~~ didn't break through. The captain sighed ~~and walked back to the crew~~. The crew cheered ~~because they were so happy~~. They were safe.

After expanding and tightening, look at your words. Find general, nondescriptive words and replace them with more specific ones. Look at this sentence:

Colorful flowers grew in the garden.

Colorful, flowers, and grew are very general words. They don't show the reader exactly what the garden looks like. Can you make the words more specific? Are the flowers daisies? Tulips? What color are the flowers? Are there a lot or just a few? This sentence creates a better picture for the reader:

Bright orange zinnias crowded the garden.

Proofreading

Another part of the revising process is proofreading. This is when you check your piece for mistakes in grammar, spelling, and punctuation. You can use a dictionary to look up the meaning of words. You can also use a thesaurus to find more descriptive words. Your computer has these tools, too.

Finally, you can check your spelling on the computer. Remember, though, that the computer spell checker doesn't catch all mistakes. The words in the following sentence are spelled correctly, but some are the wrong words to use. The computer won't find the mistakes. Can you?

The kids red there books quietly.

Time to Share

Now you can let readers peek into your backpack! Don't wait until you are done writing to show someone else. Get some advice! Even professional authors don't write alone. They get advice from other writers during all steps of the process. Author and illustrator Tomie dePaola gets advice from his editor when he has an idea. "We bounce it around like a ball, all over the place, adding new stuff, rejecting other stuff," he says.[5]

A writing partner can be a lifesaver. Peer review

Who can give you good advice about writing? Your friends!

is when you trade papers with a classmate or friend, or read your work to a group. Your partner's or group's feedback will improve your writing.

A peer reviewer might point out something that worked well. She might say, "I could tell Joe was shy because he always hid in the closet." Then she'll point out ways to improve your story. She might say, "You said Annie was rich, so I wanted you to give me more details about her house and her clothes." A peer reviewer might also use a rubric. This is a list of requirements that your teacher expects from the assignment.

Bookmaking

Here is how to make a blank book:

1. Fold about ten sheets of plain white paper in half.
2. Fold one piece of colorful paper in half. This is your cover.
3. Slip the white pages inside the cover.
4. Secure the pages to the cover with a ribbon or staples.
5. Fill your book with your creative writing and share it with readers!

Giving other people feedback on their work helps you, too. It is a great way to practice being a writer. You learn what works and doesn't work. You can use what you learn the next time you write something.

After you get feedback, you might have to revise your work again. In fact, you'll probably need to revise many times before your piece is done. Jane Yolen says, "If I ever write the perfect book, I'll stop writing."[6]

Revising is practice. The more you write, the more practice you get. The more practice, the better your writing! Your piece is done when you can't find any more mistakes and you feel your ideas are easy to understand.

Now it's time to share your ideas with the world. This is called publishing. You can entertain an audience by reading your piece aloud. You can give it to someone as a gift. Some kids get their work published in magazines. Web sites post kids' stories, too. Always check with an adult to see if a site is safe. You can even make your work into a book and keep it on your shelf.

You don't have to share your work. It's okay if you want to write memories, stories, and poems just for yourself. A diary, also called a journal, is a great type of creative writing.

Now that you've emptied your backpack, strap it back on and head out. It's time to collect some new ideas!

Glossary

buildup—The part of a story when the character struggles with a problem.

characters—The people, animals, or objects in a story.

character sketch—A description of a character's appearance and personality. This description helps a writer learn more about the character before starting to write.

climax—The most important or exciting moment in the story, when the problem or mystery is solved.

compare and contrast—To identify how two things are alike and different.

creative writing—Writing meant to entertain readers. Three types are personal narratives, fiction stories, and poems.

descriptive—Using lots of details to tell exactly what someone or something is like.

details—Small bits of information that tell a reader more about your subject, such as what something looks like, or how someone acts or feels.

dialogue—Words that characters say when they speak directly to each other.

drafting—Creating the first version of your piece of writing.

editor—The person at a publishing company who helps revise an author's work and make it into a book.

expanding—Adding more information and details.

feedback—Someone else's opinions or thoughts about your work.

fiction story—Writing that you make up with your imagination, often in the form of sentences and paragraphs.

graphic organizers—Charts and diagrams that writers use to plan and organize their work.

metaphor—A comparison without using *like* or *as*.

mood—The feeling of a piece of writing, such as scary or silly or sad.

narrator—The character who tells a story.

peer review—Sharing your work with other writers to see what they think.

personal narrative—Writing that describes an experience in your own life.

plagiarism—Using someone else's words as if they were your own, without giving credit to the original writer or speaker.

plot—What happens in a story.

poem—A piece of writing that uses words in artistic ways to describe an object or situation. Many poems have rhythm, rhyme, repetition, and strong images.

prewriting—Organizing your ideas before drafting your piece of writing.

proofreading—Rereading your piece to fix spelling, grammar, and punctuation mistakes.

publishing—Sharing your completed work with other people in a printed book, online article, or other form.

repetition—Using a word or phrase more than once.

research—Hunting for information about a certain topic.

revising—Adding, taking away, replacing, or moving around words to improve your piece of writing.

rhyme—The use of the same vowel sound in more than one word, such as *car* and *far*.

rhythm—A regular beat, as in music.

rubric—A check-off list that tells a writer what is expected from an assignment.

setting—Where and when a story takes place.

similes—Comparisons using the word *like* or *as*.

suspense—A feeling of wanting to know what happens next.

tense—The form of a verb that tells readers if the action happens in the past, present, or future.

theme—The main message or point of a piece of writing.

thesaurus—A reference book or computer tool that lists a word along with other words that have the same, or similar, meaning.

tightening—Taking out unnecessary words while revising.

Chapter Notes

1. Jane Yolen, "For Writers," Jane Yolen, n.d., <www.janeyolen.com/forwrtrs.html> (September 22, 2008).

2. Gail Carson Levine. *Writing Magic: Creating Stories That Fly* (New York: Collins, 2006), p. 5.

3. Kate DiCamillo, "On Writing," *Kate DiCamillo*, 2008, <www.katedicamillo.com/onwrit2.html> (September 22, 2008).

4. Barry Lane, *After the End: Teaching and Learning Creative Revision* (Portsmouth, N.H.: Heinemann, 1992), p. 22.

5. Tomie dePaola, "Creative Process," *Tomie dePaola*, n.d., <www.tomie.com/being_an_artist/creative_process.html> (September 22, 2008).

6. Yolen.

Further Reading

Books

Bullard, Lisa. *You Can Write a Story! A Story-Writing Recipe for Kids.* Minnetonka, Minn.: Two-Can, 2007.

Jarnow, Jill. *Writing to Describe.* New York: PowerKids Press, 2006.

Olien, Rebecca. *Kids Write!: Fantasy & Sci Fi, Mystery, Autobiography, Adventure & More.* Charlotte, Vt.: Williamson Books, 2005.

Prelutsky, Jack. *Pizza, Pigs, and Poetry: How to Write a Poem.* New York: Collins, 2008.

Rhatigan, Joe. *Write Now!: The Ultimate, Grab-a-Pen, Get-the-Words-Right, Have-a-Blast Writing Book.* New York: Lark Books, 2005.

On the Internet

Fun Brain Kid Center
http://www.funbrain.com/words.html

Internet Public Library: KidSpace
http://www.ipl.org/div/kidspace/

Kids' Space
http://www.kids-space.org/

Index